W9-CHZ-592

SWEDEN
the culture

April Fast and Keltie Thomas

A Bobbie Kalman Book

The Lands, Peoples, and Cultures Series

Crabtree Publishing Company

www.crabtreebooks.com

The Lands, Peoples, and Cultures Series

Created by Bobbie Kalman

Coordinating editor
Ellen Rodger

Project editor
Sean Charlebois

Production coordinator
Rosie Gowsell

Project development, design, editing, and photo research
First Folio Resource Group, Inc.
  Erinn Banting
  Molly Bennett
  Tom Dart
  Alana Lai
  Jaimie Nathan
  Debbie Smith
  Anikó Szocs

Prepress and printing
Worzalla Publishing Company

Consultants
Marita Karlisch, Archivist/Librarian,
American Swedish Institute

Photographs
AFP/Corbis/Magmaphoto.com: p. 23 (left); Björn Andrén/
GreatShots: title page; Archives Charmet/Bridgeman Art
Library: p. 7 (bottom); Astrid Lindgrens Värld: p. 29 (top);
Ellen Barone/Houserstock: p. 25 (bottom); Annie Griffiths
Belt/Corbis/Magmaphoto.com: p. 23 (right) Helena
Bergengren/Tiofoto: p. 27 (top); Mikael Bertmar/Tiofoto: p. 9,
p. 11 (top); Bettmann/Corbis/ Magmaphoto.com: p. 22 (left),
p. 29 (left); Jan Butchofsky-Houser/Houserstock: p. 22 (right);
Bengt-Göran Carlsson/Tiofoto: p. 27 (bottom); Lars Dahlström/
Tiofoto: p. 16 (left); Chad Ehlers/ Tiofoto: p. 8, p. 11 (bottom);
Macduff Everton/Corbis/ Magmaphoto.com: p. 16 (right), p.
18 (both), p. 20 (left); Johan Hedenström: p. 26; Hal
Horwitz/Corbis/Magmaphoto.com: p. 3; Tham Jan/Svenska
Institutet: p. 10; Bembaron Jeremy/ Corbis Sygma/
Magmaphoto.com: p. 25 (top); Bob Krist/ Corbis/
Magmaphoto.com: p. 15 (right); Chris Lisle/Corbis/
Magmaphoto.com: p. 14; Nils-Johan Norenlind/Tiofoto:
p. 4 (left); North Wind Pictures: p. 28 (left); Pushkin Museum,
Moscow, Russia/Bridgeman Art Library: p. 15 (left); Courtesy
of the Royal Library, Stockholm: p. 28 (right); Setboun/
Corbis/Magmaphoto.com: p. 6; Ulf Sjöstedt/Tiofoto: p. 7 (top);
Staffan Widstrand/Corbis/Magmaphoto.com: p. 24 (top);
Hubert Stadler/Corbis/Magmaphoto.com: p. 13; Patrick
Trägårdh/Svenska Institutet: p. 5 (top); Trip/Tom Paley: p. 4
(right); Trip/C. Rennie: p. 20 (right); Trip/A. Tovy: p. 5
(bottom); Tomas Utsi: p. 12 (both), p. 17, p. 24 (bottom); Dan
Vander Zwalm/Corbis Sygma/Magmaphoto.com: p. 21, p. 29
(right); Bo Zaunders/Corbis/Magmaphoto.com: p. 19 (cover)

Every effort has been made to obtain the appropriate credit
and full copyright clearance for all images in this book. Any
oversights, despite Crabtree's greatest precautions, will be
corrected in future editions.

Illustrations
Sylvie Daigneault: pp. 30–31
Dianne Eastman: icon
David Wysotski, Allure Illustrations: back cover

Cover: The National Lucia Choir at Skansen. On December 13,
the eldest daughter of a Swedish family plays the role of St.
Lucia, dressed in white and crowned with candles.

Icon: The *dalahast*, or Dala horse, which appears at the head of
each section, is a well-known symbol of Sweden. The horses
are hand carved and painted with bright colors.

Title page: Girls wait to perform at a Midsummer's Eve
celebration. Midsummer, or *midsommar*, is celebrated the first
weekend after June 21 to welcome summer.

Back cover: Herring, silvery fish that grow to be 10 inches
(25 centimeters) long, swim in large schools in the Baltic Sea,
off the eastern coast of Sweden.

Note: When using foreign terms, the author has followed the
Swedish style of only capitalizing people and place names.

Published by
Crabtree Publishing Company

PMB 16A,	612 Welland Avenue	73 Lime Walk
350 Fifth Avenue	St. Catharines	Headington
Suite 3308	Ontario, Canada	Oxford OX3 7AD
New York	L2M 5V6	United Kingdom
N.Y. 10118		

Cataloging-in-Publication Data
Thomas, Keltie, 1966-
  Sweden : the culture / Keltie Thomas.
    p. cm. -- (Lands, peoples, and cultures series) "A Bobbie
Kalman Book."
Includes index.
**Summary: Text and photos show how Swedes celebrate
holidays and festivals, using art, music, and dance.**
  ISBN 0-7787-9329-X (rlb) -- ISBN 0-7787-9697-3 (pbk)
  1. Sweden--Civilization--Juvenile literature. [1. Sweden--
Civilization.] I. Title. II. Series.
DL631.T52 2004
948.5--dc22
                                        2003016183
                                        LC

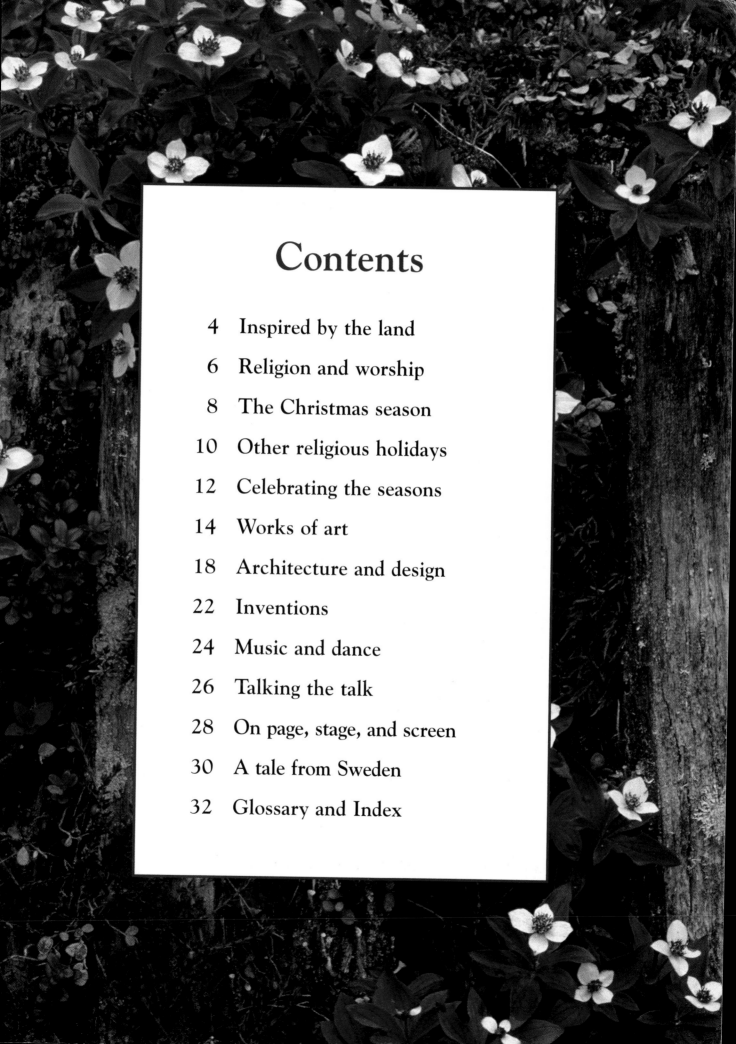

Contents

Inspired by the land

Sweden's seasons and landscape have inspired artists in this northern European country for centuries. They paint scenes of the windswept, frozen mountains, thick forests, fertile plains, and rugged coasts. Some pictures pour with light, like the light from the sun in the far north, which does not dip below the horizon for weeks during the summer. Other pictures are darker, showing the long winter days when the sun does not rise. The change of seasons also inspires writers, and is celebrated at festivals throughout the country.

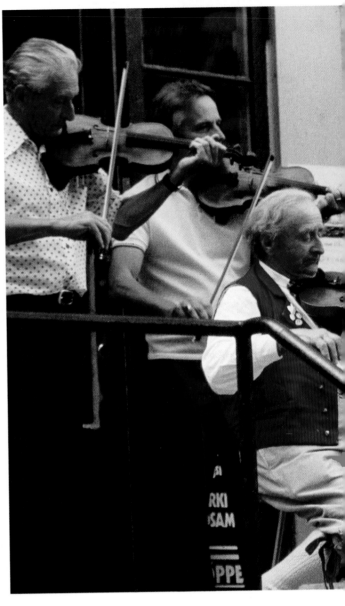

Violinists play Swedish folk music during a festival in Sundborn, a village in central Sweden.

Celebrating the south

Most Swedes live in southern cities along the coasts that were once trading ports. In these cities, musicians play modern and traditional instruments, **architects** and designers develop new ways to construct buildings and furniture, inventors create a wide range of products, from matches to cell phones, and writers and musicians tell stories about the history of their country.

On June 6, Swedes celebrate their national holiday, Flag Day. People show their pride in their country by waving flags or wearing clothing with flags on it.

Two young Sami women wear traditional clothing embroidered with brightly colored wool. The Sami are believed to be the first people to have lived in Sweden.

The Skansen Open-Air Museum in Stockholm shows visitors how Swedish people dressed, worked, and lived in the past. The outdoor museum has 150 buildings from different regions in Sweden.

Religion and worship

The Sami, who live mainly in northern Sweden, are thought to have been the first people to settle in the country, nearly 10,000 years ago. They worshiped many gods and goddesses who they believed controlled nature, such as Mattarahkka, the goddess of Earth. Today, like the majority of Swedes, many Sami practice Lutheranism, a **denomination** of Christianity. Christians believe in one God and in his son, Jesus Christ.

Some Sami incorporate the beliefs of their **ancestors** with Christian practices. For example, *noaids*, religious leaders believed to have the power to heal the sick and predict the future, often perform **rituals** during services in Sami Christian churches.

Viking worship
The Vikings, who ruled Sweden between 800 A.D. and 1050 A.D., also believed there were gods and goddesses in nature, which they called Aesir. For example, they believed that Thor, the god of thunder, protected the world from evil with a magic hammer named Mjölner. Some Swedes wear charms on necklaces or bracelets in the shape of Thor's hammer to protect them and bring them luck.

Coming of Christianity
Christian **missionaries** arrived in Sweden in 829 A.D. to teach about a denomination of Christianity called Roman Catholicism. They met with a lot of opposition from the Sami and Vikings, who did not wish to **convert**. When Olaf Skötkonung, a Viking king, ruled Sweden between 990 and 1022, he declared Roman Catholicism Sweden's official religion. If people refused to change their beliefs, they were removed from their land, beaten, and even killed. Viking **temples** were destroyed, and the Sami lost many of their traditions.

Some noaids *play drums, called* spåtrumma, *that are made of wood and animal skins. The drums have symbols of gods, goddesses, animals, and people on them. The* noaids *place pieces of bone on the drums as they play. When they stop drumming, they make predictions, such as whether a harvest will be successful, based on which symbol the bone lands on.*

Lutheranism
Roman Catholicism remained Sweden's main religion until 1544 when Gustav Vasa, king of Sweden at the time, made Lutheranism the official religion. Lutheranism is based on the teachings of Martin Luther, a German religious scholar. Martin Luther believed the Roman Catholic Church misused its power and did not make religion easy for people to follow. For example, he thought that the Bible should be printed in the languages that people spoke everyday, instead of in **Latin**, which only very educated people understood.

Freedom to choose

Until the year 2000, anyone born in Sweden was automatically made a member of the Lutheran Church. Citizens were allowed to withdraw their membership and follow any religion they chose. Today, people are not automatically Lutheran. They decide which religion they want to follow, including other denominations of Christianity, such as the Baptist Church, Anglicanism, Pentecostalism, and Roman Catholicism. People from other religious backgrounds, such as Judaism, Hinduism, Islam, and Buddhism, also worship throughout the land.

Members of a Lutheran Church listen to readings from the Bible during a Sunday church service. People also go to church for special ceremonies, such as baptisms. During a baptism, a minister pours water over a baby's head and welcomes him or her to the Church.

Sankta Birgitta

Sankta Birgitta, or Saint Brigit, is the patron **saint** of Sweden. A patron saint is a special guardian believed to protect people. Brigit was born in 1303 in Uppland, a region in east-central Sweden. In the mid 1300s, she founded the Brigittine Order, a religious group that taught people about God and helped the poor and needy. Today, nuns, who are women who devote their life to God, still belong to the Brigittine Order in Sweden and other European countries. People honor Saint Brigit on July 23, Saint Brigit's Day, by attending a special church service and holding parades in which statues of Saint Brigit are carried through the streets. Girls named after Saint Brigit are given small gifts on this day.

In 1999, Saint Brigit was made one of the six patron saints of Europe by the Pope, head of the Roman Catholic Church.

 # The Christmas season

Christmas, on December 25, celebrates the birth of Jesus Christ. Festivities last a month, from December 13, Saint Lucia Day, to January 13, Saint Knut's Day. People decorate their homes, businesses, schools, and churches with Christmas trees, lights, wreaths, cookies, candies, and ornaments made of straw. The straw ornaments are a reminder of Jesus' birth in a stable.

Saint Lucia Day

Saint Lucia, whose name means "light," was a saint born in Italy around 283 A.D. According to legend, Saint Lucia brought food to Swedish villagers who had nothing to eat on one of the darkest nights of the year. To help her find her way through the darkness, she wore a crown topped with candles.

To honor Saint Lucia, the eldest daughters in Swedish families wake up early in the morning on Saint Lucia Day, and dress in white gowns with red sashes and crowns ringed with seven candles. The crowns used to be topped with real candles, but today they are powered by batteries. Then, the girls walk through their dark homes and wake their families with songs about Saint Lucia. The girls serve a delicious breakfast of coffee and *lussekatter*, which are sweet buns flavored with raisins and a spice called saffron. The buns are baked in the shape of figure eights.

(top) On Saint Lucia Day, many Swedes attend church services where choirs of boys and girls sing. During the ceremony, one girl dressed as Saint Lucia makes a special speech to honor the saint.

8

A Christmas feast

The greatest feast of the year is on Christmas Eve. Families enjoy a *smörgåsbord*, which means "open sandwich table." A traditional *smörgåsbord* has about 40 hot and cold dishes, including *lutfisk*, or dried and salted codfish soaked in **lye**; *köttbullar*, which are Swedish meatballs made from ground beef, onions, and spices, topped with a cream sauce or gravy, and sweet and sour red cabbage. For dessert, rice pudding and *pepparkakor*, which are Christmas cookies that taste like gingerbread, are served.

Julklappar

After a large meal, it is time for *julklappar*, which means "Christmas gifts." Jultomte, the Swedish Santa Claus, knocks on the door with presents for the children. After the gifts are exchanged, people sing and tell stories until it is time for bed. On Christmas Day, they go to church, then spend a quiet day with their families.

End of the Christmas season

Saint Knut's Day honors a king from Denmark who ruled Sweden between 1080 and 1086, and a Swedish duke who lived from 1096 to 1131. King Knut was known for his kindness to the Swedish people. During his rule, he declared that the Christmas season should last one month, and people have followed the tradition ever since. Duke Knut was a much-loved leader in Sweden who was murdered because of his religious beliefs. On Saint Knut's Day, people sing songs about the two heroes and dance around the Christmas tree one last time to make the end of the Christmas season a happy event. Then, they take down the tree and decorations.

Jultomte, or Santa Claus, hands out gifts at a Swedish home in Malmö, a city in the south, on Christmas Eve.

Other religious holidays

On Easter, Christians celebrate the death and resurrection, or rebirth, of Jesus Christ. Leading up to Easter is the 40-day period of Lent. People used to fast, or give up their favorite food or drink, during Lent and they did not eat rich ingredients such as **lard** or sugar. To use up these ingredients before Lent, they made special treats such as *semlor*, which are rich rolls filled with almond paste and whipped cream. Today, few people fast during Lent and they eat *semlor* throughout Lent and Easter.

Skärtorsdag

Christian traditions and Swedish folklore are celebrated on *skärtorsdag*, or Holy Thursday, the Thursday before Easter. Hundreds of years ago, Swedish Christians gave money to the poor on Holy Thursday. Swedes combined this tradition with a Viking belief that witches flew to meet the **devil** on this day. Some people lit fires or set off firecrackers to scare the witches away. Today, children dress as good Easter witches in tattered clothes, head scarves, and face paint. They carry broomsticks and pots door to door and politely ask for change or candy.

Easter

Many Swedes celebrate Easter by going to church for a special service. After church, children come home to find birch branches decorated with colorful feathers and with eggs filled with candies. People used to believe that the birch twigs sped up the arrival of spring. In the evening, families gather for a meal of roast lamb, and a dessert of candy and *semlor*.

All Saints' Day and All Souls' Day

In many countries, people celebrate All Saints' Day on November 1 and All Souls' Day on November 2. All Saints' Day honors all Christian saints, and All Souls' Day honors friends and family members who have died. In Sweden, people celebrate both holidays on the first Saturday of November. People gather in churches lit with candles and decorated with wreaths to remember their loved ones. They also visit cemeteries and leave special lanterns on people's graves that burn well into the night.

Three Easter witches pretend to ride a broomstick on skärtorsdag.

A young girl paints hard-boiled eggs in preparation for Easter. Children paint different patterns, shapes, and animals on the eggs and then eat them Easter morning.

A cemetery outside Stockholm is lit up by lanterns and candles placed on people's graves on All Souls' Day.

Celebrating the seasons

The arrival of winter, spring, summer, and fall are cause for great celebration in Sweden. People gather to sing, dance, eat, and enjoy traditions that date back to the time of their ancestors.

Kiruna Snow Festival

Each January, the small town of Kiruna, in the far north, holds the largest snow festival in Europe. Sculptors from around the world create life-sized ice sculptures and magnificent snow castles. The Sami, who live in Kiruna, hold a fashion show that displays traditional clothing made of woven fabric dyed bright red, yellow, blue, and green. The fabric is carefully **embroidered** with geometric patterns, flowers, and other designs. People also watch dog, sled, and snowmobile races that take place throughout the town. When the races are over and it is time to warm up, people enjoy food and drinks served inside domed houses made from snow that are built for the festival.

A Sami woman sells colorful clothing at the Jokkmokk Market.

Jokkmokk Market

The Sami in the town of Jokkmokk, just north of the **Arctic Circle**, hold a winter market each February. The market began 400 years ago when Sami reindeer herders gathered to trade their hides and furs. Today, Sami craftspeople sell handmade items, such as knives with handles made from reindeer bones and antlers, and light baskets woven from birch, fir, and willow roots. The highlight of the market is a reindeer race on a frozen lake. Everyone gathers on the shore to watch the race as they drink black coffee flavored with salt and sing traditional songs called *joiks*.

Artists carve large blocks of snow and ice for the Kiruna Snow Festival.

Valborgsmässöafton

After a long winter, spring is welcomed with a lively festival on April 30, called *valborgsmässöafton*, or Walpurgis Night. People light large bonfires, sometimes even leaping through the flames for luck. They listen to choirs and toss their winter hats into rivers as a symbol that winter is over. The tradition of lighting fires began when the Vikings burned bonfires to scare **predators** and evil spirits away from their herds of cattle and sheep, which they had let out of their barns for the first time after the winter.

Midsommar

Midsommar, or Midsummer, is celebrated on the weekend after June 21 to welcome summer. Some celebrations in the north last all night because the sun does not set. People gather to sing, play fiddles and accordions, and eat a large meal of herring and potatoes, which are both in season. Many Swedes believe in superstitions surrounding the arrival of summer. Some girls believe that if they pick seven different flowers and put them under their pillow on Midsummer's Eve, they will dream about the person they will marry.

Families dressed in traditional Swedish clothes enjoy a picnic at a midsommar celebration in northern Sweden.

Works of art

Some of the earliest examples of Swedish art are petroglyphs, or rock carvings, found on rocks in western and southern Sweden. The carvings, which are more than 3,000 years old, show warriors, ships, and people hunting and fishing. **Archaeologists** have also found axes, swords, shields, bowls, platters, and cups made by the Vikings. The Vikings decorated these items with pictures of interlocking shapes, gods and goddesses, animals, and Viking heroes, such as the brave warrior Loki.

Kurbits painting

A type of folk painting called *kurbits* became popular in the mid 1700s. *Kurbits* was also known as Dala painting because it originated in the Dala region of central Sweden. Artists used bold shapes painted in bright colors to portray scenes from everyday life, such as farmers working in fields, animals, and landscapes.

(top) On the Swedish island of Gotland, in the Baltic Sea, large boulders are arranged to look like a Viking longship. The Vikings sailed longships through rough ocean waters to the lands they conquered.

Country Festival, *by Anders Zorn, shows people dancing at a* midsommar *celebration.*

Watercolor and natural light

In the late 1800s, a style of painting called *plein-air*, which means "open air" in French, gained popularity in Sweden. The watercolor paintings captured scenes from everyday life and the beauty of the Swedish countryside. Carl Larsson (1853–1919) painted scenes of his home life and of people in the village where he lived. Anders Zorn (1860–1920) painted people from Dalarna, the region in central Sweden where he lived, and portraits of Swedish and world leaders.

Swedish sculptors

Swedish sculptors have created works of art for display in Sweden and around the world. Carl Eldh (1873–1954) sculpted the *Olympic Runners* outside a stadium in Stockholm and a series of sculptures in the gardens of Stockholm's city hall. Carl Milles (1875–1955) made monuments and statues of bronze, stone, and wood. Many of his statues stand in Millesgården, or Milles Park, in Stockholm.

An underground art gallery

Stockholm's subway line, Tunnelbanan, doubles as an art gallery. When it was built in the 1940s, architects designed the 65-mile- (110-kilometer-) long subway line so each station could be used to display paintings, **installations**, sculptures, and **mosaics**. Some stations, such as the *Grottstationer*, or "Cave Station," were made to look like natural caves.

Blue patterns inspired by Sweden's north decorate the ceiling of Grottstationer, *or "Cave Station," in Tunnelbanan.*

Swedish crafts

Dalarna, the area where Dala painting began, is also well known for its brightly painted wooden chairs, chests, tabletops, dolls, and *dalahast*, or Dala horses. *Dalahast* were first made by artists in the 1700s to honor horses in the region that pulled heavy loads of **timber**. The small carvings of the horses are decorated with different patterns and painted in red, yellow, blue, black, and white. Most people in Sweden have at least one *dalahast* in their homes.

Two glassblowers make a bowl at the Kosta Boda glassworks.

A craftsperson carefully paints a dalahast, or Dala horse. Traditionally, the horses were carved and painted during the long fall and winter evenings when it was too dark to work outside.

Fragile art

Sweden developed a reputation for making fine crystal and glassware in the 1700s. Crystal is a special type of glass with **minerals** that make it sparkle when light hits it. The first Swedish glassworks were opened in Stockholm, but were moved to the wooded Småland Highlands, in southeastern Sweden, because there were more trees there to fuel the hot fires needed to blow the glass. Today, Småland is nicknamed "the Kingdom of Crystal" because of the almost 20 glassworks there. These glassworks include Kosta Boda, founded in 1742, which is the oldest glassworks in Sweden. The factory makes handmade crystal and glass that is sold throughout the world.

Sami handicrafts

The Sami use the antlers, bones, and hides of the reindeer they herd to make everyday items and traditional crafts. Needles made from reindeer bones are used to sew warm clothing, shoes, blankets, and tents made from reindeer hides. Sculptures and carvings are made from reindeer antlers. Many Sami sell these traditional handicrafts in shops and at fairs, markets, and festivals.

A Sami craftsperson carves reindeer antlers into knife handles. Once the handles are shaped, geometric shapes and pictures of Sami gods and goddesses are carved onto them.

Many of Sweden's cities have buildings that date back hundreds of years. Visby, a city on the island of Gotland, began as a Viking trading port. In the **Middle Ages**, it grew into a German merchant town. Because of its well-preserved stone houses and other buildings from the 1200s and 1300s, Visby was declared a World Heritage Site by the United Nations Educational, Scientific, and Cultural Organization (UNESCO).

Kalmar Slott, or Kalmar Castle, was built near water to protect it from attackers. A thick wall surrounded the castle, and a moat, or deep ditch filled with water, prevented people who climbed the wall from entering.

The nearly four-mile- (six-kilometer-) long wall that rings Visby was built in the 1200s by merchants who wished to protect their belongings and families. Most of the wall is in ruins, but the gate, through which all visitors had to pass, still stands today.

Castles

Sweden's kings and queens built castles to protect their families and riches from **invaders** and pirates. Kalmar Slott, or Kalmar Castle, towers over the waters on the southeastern coast of Sweden. The enormous castle began as a tower used to defend Kalmar's port from pirates in the 1100s. Through the 1200s and 1300s, when it was the part-time residence of the king and other members of the royal family, the castle was expanded to include hundreds of rooms, **battlements** from which soldiers shot arrows at attackers, and a surrounding wall. The king's quarters, which is decorated with an enormous **mural** of a fox hunt, has a secret passageway. The passageway leads to other parts of the castle so that the king could escape and hide elsewhere during an attack.

Kungliga Slottet

In 1252, Swedish ruler Birger Jarl built a large **fort** on the island of Stadsholmen, in the east. The fort eventually grew into the modern-day city of Stockholm, which now extends over fourteen islands. Sweden's royal palace, Kungliga Slottet, stands on the site of Birger Jarl's fort. The castle, which has 608 rooms, is the largest castle in the world. The rooms are decorated with **tapestries**, paintings of former Swedish rulers, and elegant furniture.

The Cathedral of Lund

Construction of the Cathedral of Lund, in the south, began in the 1080s. The **cathedral** has imposing sandstone towers and an ornate clock. Each day at noon, wooden figures of the Three Wise Men, who visited Baby Jesus on the night he was born, come out of the clock while music plays. The inside and outside of the cathedral are decorated with carvings and stained glass windows depicting Swedish monarchs, heroes, and people from the Bible.

Kungliga Slottet, the royal palace in Stockholm, is home to the royal family, and is also used for special ceremonies, such as welcoming leaders from other countries.

Church villages

Gammelstad, or "Old Town," in the east, is one of the few remaining church villages in Europe. In the 1400s, small cottages were built near churches. People in the countryside, who traveled long distances to attend services, spent the night in these cottages before traveling home the next morning. The town was made a World Heritage Site in 1996.

Kiruna Kyrka

In the far north, Sami who practice Christianity pray at Kiruna Kyrka, or Kiruna Church. The church was built between 1909 and 1912 to look like the traditional tents the Sami used when **migrating** with their reindeer herds. Its exterior is painted bright red and is made up of two buildings — the church and a bell tower. Inside the church is a large painting, which was done by Sweden's Prince Eugen (1865–1947). It shows a group of Sami with Julieboo, the first priest of Kiruna Kyrka.

The red brick Stadshuset has a 450-foot- (137-meter-) high tower capped with three golden crowns.

Modern architecture

Swedish architect Ragnar Östberg (1866–1945) is known for his design of Stadshuset, Stockholm's city hall. Stadshuset is constructed around two courtyards, the uncovered Borgargården and the covered Blå Hallen, which has a ceiling that looks like an overturned Viking **longship**. The Golden Hall, used as a banquet hall, is decorated with more than eighteen million tiles made of gold, glass, and ceramic that show scenes from Swedish history.

The tombstone of the founder of Kiruna is built into the base of Kiruna Kyrka's bell tower.

Functional first

Two Swedish designers, Erik Gunnar Asplund and Gregor Paulsson, introduced a new idea to design, called functionalism, in 1930. Functionalism is a simple style that uses common materials, such as wood, metal, and plastic, to create objects that are attractive and useful. The idea of functionalism became popular with other Swedish designers, who created everything from buildings to musical instruments to furniture.

Comfort and simplicity

Functionalism drastically changed the design of furniture in both Sweden and around the world. Bruno Mathsson (1907–1988) used materials such as birch, leather, and steel to design chairs.

His two most famous chairs are Pernilla, the "relaxing chair," and Eva, the "working chair." They are similar in design, with sleek wood that forms the legs and sweeps up to become armrests, but Pernilla is lower and has a foot rest, while Eva fits comfortably behind a desk.

Ingvar Kamprad (1926–) is the best known designer of functionalist furniture. In the 1950s, he introduced foldable furniture, such as chairs and tables, that could be transported or stored easily. The idea led him to begin the company IKEA, which continues to sell affordable, simple furniture and housewares based on functionalist designs.

A designer at an IKEA office looks at catalogs of functionalist-inspired furniture and housewares.

Inventions

Swedes have designed many products that are used around the world today. These inventions have improved industry, health, and everyday life. Alfred Nobel (1833–1896), for example, invented dynamite in 1866. His discovery allowed miners and builders to blast tunnels through rock and mountains. This made it easier to extract the country's **natural resources** and build railways and roads.

After Alfred Nobel died, the money he earned from inventing dynamite was used to fund a prize called the Nobel Prize. The Nobel Prize is awarded to people who make significant contributions in medicine, literature, peace, economics, and certain sciences.

Safety matches

Gustaf Erik Pasch (1788–1862) was a **chemistry** professor who invented the safety match in 1844. Pasch removed the **flammable** part of the head of a match and added it to the striking surface on matchboxes. That way, matches could ignite only if they were struck against the striking surface, not if they struck against one another.

All in one

Modern telephone design owes much to Lars Magnus Ericsson (1846–1926). In the mid 1800s, phones had two separate parts: a mouthpiece to speak into and a speaker used to hear. Ericsson was the first person to attach the mouthpiece and speaker with a handle, the way telephones are designed today. In 1876, he founded the Ericsson company, which still designs telephones and other communications equipment.

More than two-thirds of Swedes own cell phones, many of which are designed by the Ericsson company, in Sweden.

Improved packaging

Tetra Paks were invented in 1944 by Erik Wallenberg and Ruben Rausing. The paper and plastic packaging, which was first used as a container for cream, did not leak and was unbreakable. It could also be **insulated** with metals such as aluminum so food and drinks could be shipped over greater distances without going bad if they were not refrigerated.

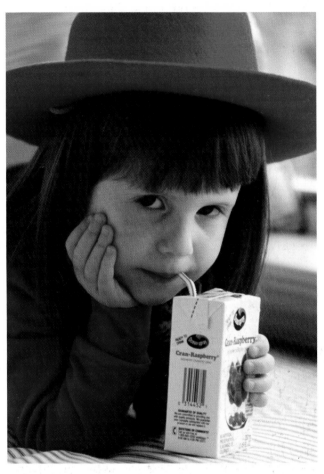

Tetra Paks were invented in Sweden and are now used in countries around the world.

Nils Bohlin demonstrates his invention, the three-point seatbelt, at a Volvo conference. In 1959, Volvo was the first carmaker to use the seatbelts.

The zipper

Zippers, used on clothing, shoes, furniture, and luggage, were originally used on galoshes, or rubber boots worn over shoes to protect them from water. The zipper was invented by Peter Aronsson and Gideon Sundbäck in 1913. At first, it had many names, such as the hookless fastener, the separable fastener, the sliding clasp, and the clasp-locker. It was finally given its name by an American named B.F. Goodrich because of the "zipping" sound it made when done up. Goodrich, who used the Swedish invention to make galoshes, later founded the American tire company B.F. Goodrich.

Medical breakthrough

Pacemakers are electronic devices that help the human heart beat regularly. The first pacemaker placed in a person's body was invented in Stockholm in 1958. It was created by surgeon Ake Senning and engineer Rune Elmqvist. The pacemaker was placed in the abdomen because it was too large to fit into the chest. Today, pacemakers are much smaller and are implanted in the chest.

Music and dance

Each region of Sweden has its own style of folk music played on fiddles, harps, accordions, bagpipes, *nyckelharpor*, and *lurs*. *Nyckelharpor,* or key fiddles, look like violins but have wooden keys on the neck of the instrument, under the strings. *Lurs* are long trumpets made of birch wood traditionally played by Sami women as they herded reindeer and cattle.

Sami music

Joiks are high-pitched songs sung by Sami herders and performed at celebrations. Most *joiks* are about people or places and are made up on the spot. They are sung without instruments to accompany them. *Laavloe* are ancient songs that have been passed down from generation to generation. Many tell stories about Sami heroes and history. *Laavloe* singers are accompanied by Sami fiddles, flutes, and clarinets.

(top) Nyckelharpor *players produce different notes by pushing down different combinations of keys and playing the strings with a bow.*

Three Sami men sing a lively joik *at a festival in Karesuando, in the north.*

Rock and pop

Many Swedish rock and pop artists have earned international reputations. The most famous group is ABBA, whose music blends disco and pop. Other well-known Swedish pop and rock groups include Roxette, Ace of Base, Eagle Eye Cherry, and the Cardigans. Most of the groups perform and record their songs in English.

Come dance!

Swedes dance to all types of music. Some, such as waltzes, polkas, and mazurkas, come from other countries. Others, such as the *långdans*, originated in Sweden. The *långdans* is performed by people who dance in a row, following certain steps such as turning and stepping toward and away from one another. Many towns have folk festivals during the summer months where folk dancers, singers, and fiddlers perform in town squares, **pubs**, and dance clubs.

Nina Persson, lead singer of the Cardigans, performs in Berlin, Germany.

Most Swedish towns have folk dancing clubs that people attend every week to practice their steps.

Talking the talk

Swedish is the official language of Sweden. It is related to German and Norwegian. In parts of Sweden, people speak different dialects, or versions, of Swedish, such as Gutniska, Svea, and Jamska. Some dialects, such as Svea, are almost identical to Swedish but have different pronunciations for certain words. Others combine words from two languages. Finno-Swedish, for example, combines Finnish and Swedish.

A longer alphabet

The Swedish alphabet is very similar to the English alphabet, but it does not have the letter "w," and there are 28 letters instead of 26. The additional letters are "å" which sounds like "oa" in "boat," "ä" which sounds like "e" in "bet," and "ö" which sounds like "oo" in "book."

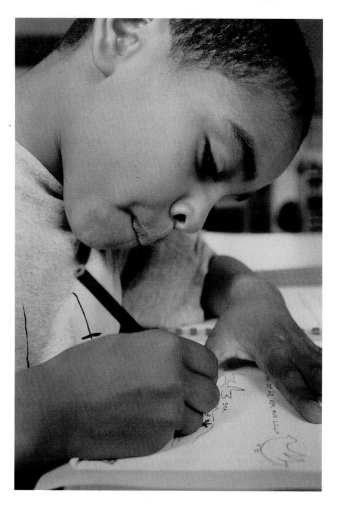

A student in Stockholm writes a story in Swedish.

Speaking Swedish

Swedish and English originally came from the same language, so some words sound the same. For example, *fisk*, *hus*, *rum*, and *man* mean "fish," "house," "room," and "man." Some modern English words have also made their way into Swedish, for example, *ett par jeanns* means "pair of jeans."

Swedish	English
Hej.	Hello.
Hejda.	Goodbye.
Goddag.	Good day.
Hu mår du?	How are you?
Tack.	Please/Thank you.
Var sa god.	You're welcome.
Ja.	Yes.

The Sami language

The main dialect of Sami spoken in Sweden is Central Sami. It is related to Finnish. Central Sami has many words that describe the same thing. For example, *sahpah* and *saevrie* are both words for snow, but one means light snow and the other means thick snow. Central Sami was traditionally passed down orally from one generation to the next. Today, the Sami are writing their stories and history in their language, and Sami is now taught in schools.

Many languages

Swedish students study both Swedish and English in school. When they reach the sixth grade, they also learn another language, such as French, German, or Spanish. In the northeast are communities of people originally from Finland. People there speak Finnish and Finno-Swedish. In the 1970s and 1980s, people from other countries, such as Turkey, Iran, Italy, and Greece, came to Sweden. Many people from these countries speak their native language at home and take classes in the language at school.

(left) A father reads to his children in Swedish. Sweden is not the only country where people speak Swedish. Swedes who have moved to countries such as the United States and Canada also speak the language.

(below) New families in Sweden often continue to speak their language at home while they learn Swedish. More than 200 languages are spoken in Sweden today.

Sweden has a rich history and tradition of folklore. The Sami and Vikings told the first tales of heroes, battles, and **mythological** creatures. Many of these stories have inspired modern poets, novelists, and **screenwriters**.

Many Viking stories are about Thor, the god of thunder, and his hammer, Mjolner, which returned to him after he threw it to earth.

Swedish poetry

Verner von Heidenstam (1859–1940) is one of Sweden's most famous poets. His first book of poems, published in 1888, was called *Pilgrimage and Wander Years*. Von Heidenstam also wrote stories and books about the history and hopes of the Swedish people. He won the Nobel Prize for literature in 1916. Karin Boye (1900–1941) also wrote poetry and fiction. Her collections of verse, such as *Moln*, reflected her sadness and the struggles in her life.

Novelists and playwrights

Scenes from Sweden's rich history are the topic of many novels. Frans G. Bengtsson (1853–1925) wrote *The Long Ships*, a novel about the raids, conquests, and adventures of a Viking who traveled to Spain, Denmark, England, and Russia. Vilhelm Moberg (1898–1973) wrote four books that form *The Emigrant Cycle*. The novels tell the story of a Swedish family that moved to Minnesota during the 1840s. August Strindberg (1849–1912) wrote short stories and novels, but he was best known for his plays, which criticized Swedish society. His realistic dialogue in plays such as *Miss Julie, A Dream Play*, and *The Father* often shocked audiences.

In addition to writing short stories, novels, and plays, August Strindberg worked as a journalist and librarian.

Pippi Longstocking is so popular in Sweden that there is an amusement park dedicated to her. Actors at the park dress up like Pippi Longstocking and other characters from the book.

Children's stories

Selma Lagerlöf (1858–1940) was the first woman to win the Nobel Prize for literature, in 1909. She wrote many novels and poems, but her most famous work is *The Wonderful Adventures of Nils*, a children's story about a boy who travels across Sweden on the back of a goose. Her stories were inspired by Viking legends and history.

Astrid Lindgren (1907–2002) is Sweden's most celebrated author. Her children's book *Pippi Longstocking* tells of the adventures of an independent, red-haired orphan. *Pippi Longstocking* has been translated into more than 75 languages and is read by children around the world.

Screen stars

In the 1920s, Swedish actors and directors made silent films that became popular in Europe and North America. Many actors and directors moved to the United States and eventually made films with dialogue. Actress Greta Garbo (1905–1990) played a ballerina who fell in love with a baron in the 1933 film *Grand Hotel*. Ingrid Bergman (1915–1982) starred in films such as *Casablanca* and *Notorious*. Ingmar Bergman (1918–) is a well-known director whose films, such as *Persona*, *Cries and Whispers*, and *Fanny and Alexander*, tell about his hopes and fears.

Swedish actors continue to have success in their country and abroad. Max von Sydow (1929–) starred in Ingmar Bergman's films *The Seventh Seal* and *Hour of the Wolf*, as well as in more recent films such as *Minority Report*.

Ingmar Bergman's more than 40 films have a dream-like quality that has inspired directors around the world.

A tale from Sweden

Many Swedish folktales are about magical creatures, such as fairies, ghosts, and wicked trolls. Some Swedish stories tell of heroes who fight the trolls. Many heroes are mighty warriors, but some are children just like you!

Olle and the troll

Olle lived in a *stuga*, or cottage, in the woods with his mother, father, and their five goats. Each day, when his parents went to work, Olle played at home.

One day, when Olle's mother and father returned home from work, they found that their goats were gone. Olle's father sighed, "A wicked old troll from the mountain has been stealing people's goats. Olle, watch out for him when we're at work. He is very dangerous. He has bushy eyebrows, a terrible grin, and a nose as big and twisted as a turnip. Instead of a left hand, he has a wolf's paw."

The very next day, there was a knock on the door. It was the troll dressed up in regular clothing, with a bandage wrapped around his left hand to disguise the wolf's paw. Olle stuck his head out the window to talk to the stranger.

"My mother and father warned me to stay inside so that I'll be safe from the troll," Olle explained.

"Well, do I look like an old troll to you?" the troll asked.

"Oh no," Olle said. "You look like a man. I'm not afraid of you. Besides, I made weapons to defend myself if the troll comes here."

Olle told the troll about his parents' stolen goats. "I happen to know where the troll keeps his stolen goats. Would you like me to take you there?" the troll asked.

Olle was excited. He wanted to get the goats back and surprise his parents. He grabbed a piece of bread, just in case he became hungry on the long walk.

After a while, Olle sat down to eat some of his bread. He broke off a piece and offered it to the troll, but the troll refused. Trolls could not accept anything from someone they wanted to harm. Olle felt bad the troll was not eating, so he popped a piece of bread into the troll's mouth.

As soon as he swallowed the bread, the troll felt different. No one had ever been nice to him before. He decided to return Olle's kindness and pulled out a small pipe on which he played a lovely tune. As he played, hundreds of goats came out of the forest.

"My parents' goats! The villagers' goats!" Olle cried. Then, he turned around to thank the troll, but he was gone.

Olle ran home with the goats as quickly as he could. When his parents saw him coming, they hurried out to hug him.

Olle breathlessly told them what had happened. "A man helped me find our goats and the goats of all the villagers."

"Olle, what did the man look like?" Olle's mother asked. "He had big eyebrows, but they were not bushy," Olle replied. "He had a large grin, but it was not wicked. He had an enormous nose, but it was not a turnip. He also did not have a wolf's paw for a left hand. His hand was bandaged up because it was hurt."

"Olle," said his mother, "that was the evil troll in disguise! How did you keep him from hurting you?"

"I shared my roll with him," Olle explained.

Olle's parents smiled. "I guess all he wanted was for someone to be nice to him." Then, Olle, his parents, and the goats headed inside.

# Glossary

ancestor A person from whom one is descended

archaeologist A person who studies the past by looking at buildings and artifacts

architect A designer of buildings

Arctic Circle An imaginary circle on the surface of the earth surrounding the North Pole

battlement A low wall at the top of a fort or castle

cathedral A large church

chemistry A branch of science that studies how substances mix and react

convert To change one's religion

denomination An organized religious group within a faith

devil An evil spirit believed to be God's enemy, according to the Christian church

embroider To make a design in cloth using thread

flammable Describing something that burns easily

fort A strong building constructed to resist attacks

installation Art created for a specific site, which may include sound, writing, and drama

insulate To use material that prevents the flow of heat into or out of an object

invader A person who enters using force

lard The fat of a pig used for cooking

Latin The language of the ancient Romans

longship A long, narrow ship used by Vikings

lye A liquid obtained by soaking wood ashes in water

Middle Ages A period in history from 500 A.D. to 1500 A.D.

migrate To move seasonally from one place to another

mineral A naturally occurring, non-living substance obtained through mining

missionary A person who travels to a foreign country to spread a particular religion

mosaic A picture or design made of small pieces of stone, glass, or tile

mural A painting created on a wall or ceiling

mythological Relating to tradional stories about gods, goddesses, or other beings with supernatural powers

natural resource A material found in nature, such as oil, coal, minerals, or timber

predator An animal that eats other animals

pub A place that sells alcoholic drinks

ritual A religious ceremony in which steps must be followed in a certain order

saint A person through whom God has performed miracles, according to the Christian Church

screenwriter A person who writes film scripts

tapestry A heavy, decorative weaving meant for hanging on walls

temple A building used for religious ceremonies

timber Wood used to construct buildings, furniture, and other objects

Index